LIVING IN HOPE

Living in
HOPE

David Pawson

Terra Nova Publications

Published in Great Britain by
Terra Nova Publications International Ltd.
Orders and enquiries: PO Box 2400 Bradford on Avon BA15 2YN
Registered Office (not for trade):
21 St.Thomas Street, Bristol BS1 6JS

Cover design by Roger Judd

ISBN 978 1 901949 60 5

Printed in Denmark by
Nørhaven Paperback A/S, Viborg

PREFACE

This book is based on a series of talks which I delivered. Originating as it does from the spoken word, its style will be found by many readers to be somewhat different from my usual written style. It is hoped that this will not detract from the substance of the biblical teaching found here.

As always, I ask the reader to compare everything I say or write with what is written in the Bible and, if at any point a conflict is found, always to rely upon the clear teaching of scripture.

David Pawson

Contents

1

THE SIGNS OF HIS COMING

(Matthew 24)

Of faith, hope and love, the greatest is love, but the rarest is hope. We Christians are to be a community of love, even though we live in a world where there is hatred, suspicion, fragmentation and broken relationships. We are to be a community of faith. We are also called to be a community of hope, in a world full of cynicism, pessimism and despair; a world that is full of agnostics, atheists, animists, polytheists and the rest.

The biblical word 'hope' does not mean wishful thinking. If I were to say 'I hope it will not rain tomorrow' that would be pure wishful thinking, especially in the English climate. Christian hope has a far stronger meaning. If the symbol of Christian faith is a cross, then the symbol of Christian hope is an anchor. We are going to need hope very much in the days that lie ahead, for a mood of pessimism is going to sweep through this nation, and God's people are called to be a people of hope who know where they are going, who know how it is all going to end, and who remain calm when everybody else is bewildered.

In Matthew chapters 24 and 25, Jesus sought to minister hope to his disciples as he told them about the future. Matthew 25 tells us how to work it all out in practice, and that is very important, but we have to lay the foundation first. Balance is needed in Christian teaching between the objective and subjective. By this I mean that some truths are there whether we believe them or not. They are objectively true, the things that my faith, hope and love will not alter, and which the lack of my faith, hope and love will not alter either. We need the solid foundation of those objective truths —what actually is true, whether we believe it or not. Only on that foundation can we begin to build the practical application. You will find that most of the epistles of the New Testament are based on that pattern. The first half is objective truth which is true whether you believe it or not. The second half is about working it out because God has worked it in. The first three chapters of Ephesians, for example, sets out objective truth which you can do nothing to alter. If we go straight through to the second half, the subjective application of truth, then we get wrapped up in ourselves and we are constantly digging around, putting the thermometer in, then taking it out again to see how we are getting on. That kind of introspection can become a barrier to what God wants to do in the world.

Consider this passage:

"O Jerusalem, Jerusalem, you who kill the prophets and stone those sent to you, how often I have longed to gather your children together, as a hen gathers her chicks under her wings, but you were not willing. Look, your house is left to you desolate. For I tell you, you will not see me again until you say, 'Blessed is he who comes in the name of the Lord.'"

Jesus left the temple and was walking away when his disciples came up to him to call his attention to its buildings. "Do you see all these things?" he asked. "I tell you the truth, not one stone here will be left on another; every one will be thrown down."

As Jesus was sitting on the Mount of Olives, the disciples came to him privately. "Tell us," they said, "when will this happen, and what will be the sign of your coming and of the end of the age?"

Jesus answered: "Watch out that no-one deceives you. For many will come in my name, claiming, 'I am the Christ', and will deceive many. You will hear of wars and rumours of wars, but see to it that you are not alarmed. Such things must happen, but the end is still to come. Nation will rise against nation, and kingdom against kingdom. There will be famines and earthquakes in various places. All these are the beginning of birth-pains.

"Then you will be handed over to be persecuted and put to death, and you will be hated by all nations because of me. At that time many will turn away from the faith and will betray and hate each other, and many false prophets will appear and deceive many

people. Because of the increase of wickedness, the love of most will grow cold, but he who stands firm to the end will be saved. And this gospel of the kingdom will be preached in the whole world as a testimony to all nations, and then the end will come.

"So when you see standing in the holy place 'the abomination that causes desolation', spoken of through the prophet Daniel — let the reader understand — then let those who are in Judea flee to the mountains. Let no-one on the roof of his house go down to take anything out of the house. Let no-one in the field go back to get his cloak. How dreadful it will be in those days for pregnant women and nursing mothers! Pray that your flight will not take place in winter or on the Sabbath. For then there will be great distress, unequalled from the beginning of the world until now — and never to be equalled again. If those days had not been cut short, no-one would survive, but for the sake of the elect those days will be shortened. At that time if anyone says to you, 'Look, here is the Christ!' or, 'There he is!' do not believe it. For false Christs and false prophets will appear and perform great signs and miracles to deceive even

the elect—if that were possible. See, I have told you ahead of time.

"So if anyone tells you, 'There he is, out in the desert,' do not go out; or, 'Here he is, in the inner rooms,' do not believe it. For as lightning that comes from the east is visible even in the west, so will be the coming of the Son of Man. Wherever there is a carcass, there the vultures will gather.

"Immediately after the distress of those days

"'the sun will be darkened,
    and the moon will not give its light;
        the stars will fall from the sky,
    and the heavenly bodies will be shaken.'

"At that time the sign of the Son of Man will appear in the sky, and all the nations of the earth will mourn. They will see the Son of Man coming on the clouds of the sky, with power and great glory. And he will send his angels with a loud trumpet call, and they will gather his elect from the four winds, from one end of the heavens to the other.

"Now learn this lesson from the fig tree: As soon

as its twigs get tender and its leaves come out, you know that the summer is near. Even so, when you see all these things, you know that it is near, right at the door. I tell you the truth, this generation [author's note: my translation of this word is 'race', see below] *will certainly not pass away until all these things have happened. Heaven and earth will pass away, but my words will never pass away.*

"No-one knows about that day or hour, not even the angels in heaven, nor the Son, but only the Father. As it was in the days of Noah, so it will be at the coming of the Son of Man. For in the days before the flood, people were eating and drinking, marrying and giving in marriage, up to the day Noah entered the ark; and they knew nothing about what would happen until the flood came and took them all away. That is how it will be at the coming of the Son of Man. Two men will be in the field; one will be taken and the other left. Two women will be grinding with a hand mill; one will be taken and the other left.

"Therefore keep watch, because you do not know on what day your Lord will come. But understand this: If the owner of the house had known at what time of

night the thief was coming, he would have kept watch and would not have let his house be broken into. So you also must be ready, because the Son of Man will come at an hour when you do not expect him.

"Who then is the faithful and wise servant, whom the master has put in charge of the servants in his household to give them their food at the proper time? It will be good for that servant whose master finds him doing so when he returns. I tell you the truth, he will put him in charge of all his possessions. But suppose that servant is wicked and says to himself, 'My master is staying away a long time,' and he then begins to beat his fellow-servants and to eat and drink with drunkards. The master of that servant will come on a day when he does not expect him and at an hour he is not aware of. He will cut him to pieces and assign him a place with the hypocrites, where there will be weeping and gnashing of teeth."

Matthew 23:37–24:51, *NIV*

I find that people have a kind of dual attitude to the future. They have a fear of it and a fascination for it. They do want to know what is going to happen, yet at the same time they don't want to know. Let me illustrate that. Supposing I had such a strong gift of prophecy that I knew the date of your death and you could ask me the date and I would reveal it to you. Would you want to know? Even if it were to be many years ahead, would you really want to know so that you could celebrate the date every year, along with your birthday perhaps? We are told that something like seven out of ten women and six out of ten men in a fairly typical English town read their horoscope every day. The horoscope writers and the fortune tellers would be out of business if they did not give more good news than bad news because people are seeking reassurance, they want to know that life is going to get better, not worse. I was in the Champs Élysées in Paris and saw a queue of well-dressed, apparently educated French men and women, outside a shop where there was a large computer. They were feeding into it maybe five euros, along with their date, place and time of birth. The printer then churned out thirty-one pages: the next month's horoscopes to predict their future! And *Old Moore's Almanack* is still one of the best sellers.

Then there are 'think tanks', and professors of futurology. The Massachusetts Institute of Technology constantly works out the end of the world for us, telling us when the oil will run out and when the growth in population will finally really spell famine on a worldwide scale.

If there really is a dual attitude to the future in present-day society — an atmosphere in which people want to know what is going to happen, yet at the same time, on another level, do not really want to know — then that is where the people of God can come into the picture —we who first hoped in Christ.

I am amazed that those who really want to know what the future holds do not get into deep study of the Bible. Its record in prediction is pretty remarkable. Did you know that 24% of the verses in the Bible contain a prediction about the future? Prediction is a vital element in the prophetic, and the prophetic people of God must be concerned with the future. Here are some more figures which might stagger you. Altogether, 737 different future events are predicted in the Bible. I do not know of another publication that has dared to make so many predictions. Some of them are predicted up to three hundred times, so you can do a little multiplication now. Of the 737 predicted things, 596 (just over 80%) have already happened — to the letter. Some of them are so extraordinary that statistically they could never have been expected to occur. Does that make the Bible 80% accurate? No, it is 100% accurate, because everything that could have happened by now has happened.

Most of the rest of the predictions are concerned with the end of the world, and when the end of the world happens you will find that it was accurate about those too! There are fewer than twenty things predicted to happen before the Lord Jesus gets back to planet earth. (Incidentally, that is one of the events that is predicted three hundred times, and it would therefore seem to be something rather important to our hope.)

Now I am concerned that Christians, who ought to be the ones who have a clear view of the future, who know what is going to happen, are in fact very confused. In fact many are so confused that they have stopped thinking about the future and just say, 'Oh well, I'll get on with the present, that's more important,' so they miss out on the vital dimension of hope. They may be strong on faith and love, but weak on hope. God wants us to be a fully three-dimensional prophetic people.

Reluctance amongst Christians to engage with this stems in part from many weird and wonderful ideas that have been thrust on us in books, films and songs. Some Christians were brought up on charts which were presented to them as the last word. But how vulnerable we are to deception, and the Lord's concern was that we should never be deceived and never get it wrong. He knew that we would be deceived, and one of the principles that he laid down to prevent us from getting wrong ideas is this: do not trust your ears, trust your eyes, because deception will come through the ears. In relation to the future, keep watch, keep your eyes open. If you listen to everything anybody says about the second coming, you will finish up in confusion. Just keep your eyes open. That is his principle, and then he told us quite clearly and specifically what to watch for. When you see these things, fine, you will know what time it is on God's clock. He warns us against listening to other people. Watch therefore.

I will give you one illustration of the kind of misleading information that can come through the ears. It is, I believe, a false prophecy, which may have started off in a place called Port Glasgow in Scotland by a woman called Margaret Macdonald. She gave a prophecy that *before* the big trouble hit this world — and the Bible does say big trouble is coming — Christians would somehow disappear and be out of it. The technical term used was 'raptured'. From Port Glasgow came that idea, which had never been heard of before, and which no-one had ever found in the Bible before. That idea was passed to a mansion at Albury outside Guildford, a mile and a half from where I used to live. In the library at that mansion a prophetic conference was held, to which a man called J N Darby came, and he picked up that idea. From there it went on, across the Atlantic, to a man called Scofield. Now it has come back over the Atlantic in force and is to be found in writings like those of Hal Lindsey and others. Many Christians are reading about it, hearing it and getting into confusion, I believe.

Now I am going to show you what Jesus said about all this, so that you may not be confused, so that you may not be deceived, so that you will know what to look for, and trust your eyes and not your ears and see what time it is on God's clock. I mention it also because for many years, especially among circles where the Holy Spirit has been renewing people, we have seen that all sorts of speculation about the second coming emerges from time to time. Back in 1982 some people were talking about the planets lining up. Some people heard about that, and I had letters asking me what I thought about the phenomenon. I said, 'Very interesting. It has been doing that every 179 years so far, and another time won't make much difference!' Well, that event came and went without any effect, but many of God's people were disturbed, and there is nothing in my Bible about the planets lining up. There is no significance to it.

Then there are those who tell us, for example, that Jesus could come back tonight and you might wake up in the morning and your family would be gone. Notice that the apostles never used such 'pressure evangelism'. It is not scriptural.

So in this maelstrom of confused opinion, Christians are saying, 'Oh well, let's forget about the second coming. Let's just get on with building the church now.' I think that is a serious loss. In response to all these different views, it is best to go for the right view, not to withdraw from the debate, and the principle in my own life, my own study, is this: **start with what Jesus said**.

I start with Jesus' outline of the future in his teaching. I do not start anywhere else — because he is the truth. Then I find a clarity and a simplicity which many Christians, in their confusion, do not seem to find. Jesus wanted us to know. I just love the way Jesus says to us, his disciples, *'If it were not so, I would have told you.'* In this chapter he also says, *'See, I've told you ahead of it so you know.'* He did not want us to be in confusion about the future. He wanted us to be clear so we would know, and would not be upset, and would not panic, and would not rush here and there and get it off balance.

Jesus is that kind of person. He wants to tell you the things you need to know. I quoted the latter portion of Matthew 23 for this reason. It was set against the backcloth of his agony over Jerusalem, when he wept and said, *'O Jerusalem, O Jerusalem, how often would I have gathered you as a hen gathers her chicks.'* (The 'birds', which are applied metaphorically to persons of the Trinity, by the way, are these: eagle, of our Father; dove of Spirit; but Son is 'hen'. There is a sermon for preachers! If the Father is like an eagle on high who sees everything down below on earth, and if the Holy Spirit is like the dove, the nearest bird to human beings, then Jesus was speaking of himself as wanting to gather people under his wing —but they were not willing.)

Then he said this: you will not see me again until you say, *'Blessed is he who comes in the name of the Lord.'* Do you know where that quotation is from?

It is from Psalm 118 which is sung in Jerusalem during the Feast of Tabernacles. And at the Feast of Tabernacles, Zechariah the prophet said that the Christ would come. The Messiah will come at the Feast of Tabernacles and he will be King over the whole earth. In Jerusalem when they celebrate the coming of the King, the coming of the Messiah, they are singing that same verse from Psalm 118. Jesus taught that we would not see him again until we are singing it.

We should expect that he will come right on time. He came right on time at the Feast of Passover. He sent the Spirit right on time at the Feast of Pentecost, but the biggest feast of all, the Feast of Tabernacles, has not yet been fulfilled, and they celebrate in Jerusalem every year — thousands of Jews and thousands of Christians, celebrating the coming of the King. So the background is his coming, his return to Jerusalem, and it is news to some that he is not coming back to Canterbury or to Rome or to Beijing or to New York but he is coming back to Jerusalem. Where else?

As they left the temple, after Jesus had wept

openly and publicly, the disciples were not so much awed by what he had said as by their surroundings. They were looking at the stones which King Herod was already using to build the temple. There was a radio programme some time ago about King Herod's buildings which are being excavated in Caesarea. King Herod, who was not a Jew, wanted to please the Jews, and to please them he thought he would 'spring clean' their temple — rebuild it, in fact. It was still rebuilding while Jesus was alive, on a scale that is almost unimaginable. The foundation of the temple was big enough to hold thirteen English cathedrals! Some of the stones were forty feet long by four feet wide by four feet high, and weighed 110 tonnes. They had no cranes, nothing but human muscle to get those stones in place. And they were piled up. The foundation of the temple was already 120 feet high. The columns of the temple carved out of one block of stone were thirty-seven feet six inches high, and three men holding hands could just get round them. This was Herod's sop to the Jews. As they walked through the temple, the disciples were not discussing Jesus' agony or his words.

We can think of them saying: look at all this Jesus, isn't it magnificent, isn't it amazing? But Jesus said, *'not one stone will be left on another.'* Once I went to the south-west corner of the temple area, where they have excavated the stones of the temple that were thrown down, and you can actually see them. It gives me a shudder up my spine to look at something Jesus said would happen, and they have found the evidence at last. They did not know where the stones had gone. They just knew that all that was left was the platform with the Wailing Wall — the edge of the platform — but nothing on top. Not a thing on those thirteen acres is left. And they did not know where the stones had gone! Now they have been uncovered, and you can actually see the stones that the Romans somehow pushed over the edge of the platform — just lying there in one gigantic heap. But the disciples could not imagine such a thing happening, except at the end of the world. So they poured out their questions. Jesus, when will this happen? What will be the sign of your coming, and what about the end of the age? Surely you are describing a disaster that can only happen when the world comes to an end? They had missed something that Jesus tried to tell them — that, in fact, it would happen before the erection was completed. Less than forty years later, it happened and those stones were thrown down. Jesus did not want his disciples speculating about the future. He then told them what would happen at his return.

I used to be a train spotter. I wonder whether you have ever been a train spotter. I remember, as a boy of six, on the platform at Newcastle Central Station, watching the first Silver Link train come in. That was in the old days of steam locomotives. When one was waiting for a train to arrive, there were four signals to watch for: the 'distance', the 'outer home', the 'inner home' and the 'starter'. When the distance signal fell, you knew the train was in the section, it was within the last few miles. When the 'outer home' signal fell, you knew the train was much nearer. When the 'inner home' went down, you got ready for it, and when the 'starter' (the last signal at the platform) went down, then you knew if you looked up the line you would see the train in just a minute. If I may use that illustration, the teaching of Jesus encourages us to look for four signals. If you are watching for these four you will know what stage we are at. You will know how near his coming is. If you keep your eyes open you will not be thrown off balance. I want to look at these four signals.

The signals will go down with an increase in speed, so the gap between the first and second will be much longer than the gap between the third and fourth. There is an acceleration going on in this chapter. The first signal I believe has gone down. And the first signal is to be seen in the world. The second signal you will see in the church. The third signal you will see in the Middle East, and the fourth signal you will see in the sky. So the four signals are in four different places.

Signal number one is the signal in the world at large — the signal of widespread disaster. The Lord mentioned three such disasters that we will see on an increasing scale as we watch: wars, famines, earthquakes. Earthquakes are caused entirely by natural causes. Wars are caused entirely by human factors, and famines are a mixture of the two. But Jesus was saying that both from nature and human nature there will be a great increase in disasters. You can expect to keep opening your newspapers and see another war, another famine, another earthquake. The number of fatal casualties from earthquakes has increased. We have all become aware of these tectonic plates on which we live, rubbing up against each other. We now accept that fact as a normal part of life. We do not always know where the next one will be.

And war. Who in Britain would have thought, prior to 9/11, that we would be at war within such a relatively short space of time, and that our troops would be giving their blood once again. Jesus invited disciples to think about forthcoming disasters. So what is your reaction to them? We know what the world's reaction is: the world says, either, isn't it terrible, isn't it awful? — or the world does not want to know and turns quickly to the sports page. But what is the Christian's reaction? The Christian's reaction must not be that it is the end of the world. In New Zealand I wondered if I would be in an earthquake, but I have never actually had that experience. Those who have been in an earthquake say it is one of the most frightening things, and their first thought is that it is the end of the world.

Again, if suddenly you found yourself in the middle of a severe war, you could well think it was the end of the world. If you were in Chad and living in a dry place where there is not a blade of green grass, and you had nothing to eat and nothing for your children, you might well be forgiven for thinking it was the end. But Jesus taught that when you see such disasters it is not the end. It may be the beginning of the end, but it is not actually the end. So do not panic. Do not rush around and say it is the end of the world. But what you should see is that these agonising things are actually the beginning of birth pains.

Now I do not know anybody in the world who regards them as that, other than Christians. Only those who hope in Christ could say that these painful things are the beginning of birth pains — not even the beginning of death pains, but birth pains.

This is a completely different way of looking at these events, so you can afford to look at the newspapers, read about the disasters and say, 'birth pains'. Like a woman suddenly getting her first contraction, earthquakes are the contractions of a creation that is groaning and waiting for redemption. Now does that put a different light on your daily newspaper? It does not mean that you gloat. Nobody could gloat over disasters that cause such suffering. Christians will do all they can to relieve the pain caused by those sufferings. Well, they would not be worthy of the name 'Christian' if they did otherwise. But deep down they do not panic, they are not thrown off balance. They do not say it's the end of the world, they say it's the beginning of birth pains.

It is the first 'contractions' of a universe that God wants to bring to new birth. Some Christians just think that God wants to bring *people* to new birth. He does not. He wants to bring *everything* to new birth. He wants to restore all things. He wants a new earth and a new heaven. He wants new everything. He wants to *make all things new*. He just began this time with us. The first time round, he began with the earth and the heavens and then he finished with us. This time round, the new birth is beginning with us and it finishes with the heavens and the earth. So, you see, we hope in Christ and we say yes, we expect wars and famines and earthquakes, and we do not say it is the end of everything. We say it is the beginning of everything, the birth pains.

Now at each stage of the four signals there is a danger that comes in, and the danger when signal number one drops is the danger of false messiahs. Since the signal is in the world, false messiahs will be in the world, and when everything is shaking and when there are earthquakes and famines and wars around, false messiahs can have a heyday. They can exploit the insecurity of people, and they do, which is why we are seeing such people leading cults, and you are going to see many, many more false 'Christs'. The insecurity that this world now offers is going to mean that these 'messiahs' will get a real hold. Jesus said it would happen, and it does not upset me. I am sad for those who have been trapped in such cults by their own insecurity in a world in which some people are desperate for somebody to look after them, but false messiahs are the danger.

Notice that they are not a danger to the church, they are only a danger to the world. That is important, because I do not think you would listen for one moment if I came up to you and said, I am Christ. You would not listen, but I am afraid that people on the street might listen, because they are very insecure. They are not grounded in their own faith. So Jesus said: now watch out for false Christs. Many will come and claim to be the Christ.

That is signal number one, and I have to say that I believe we have seen that signal. Signal number two you will see go down in the church — that is where you will have to look for it. What is it? Well, three things that will happen on a universal scale within the church. First, universal persecution: it will be hated by all nations. That has never been true in church history. For two thousand years there have been some countries where the church is under pressure and others where it is not, such as Great Britain. We have not been under pressure for a very long time. But, I tell you, the number of countries in the world where the church is being persecuted is increasing monthly.

Some years ago I saw for myself what this could mean in an African country, and that country is now in even worse shape than it was then. I looked at the map of Africa and I thought, how many countries are left where the church is not hated? It is very few. And if you look at a map of the world and blot out every country where the church is being persecuted you will blot out 9/10ths of the world in terms of numbers of countries. There are only about 10% of the countries of the world where you are still free to have a Christian celebration. Did you know that? And the number is rapidly diminishing. Jesus taught that when you see all the church hated, when the whole church is being persecuted, that is the second signal.

Secondly, Jesus also taught that one effect of this will be a great reduction in the size of the church. There is nothing like pressure to sort people out. I heard a story from Russia several decades ago. I cannot guarantee its authenticity, but I heard it from a reliable source. One always has to check out stories coming from closed countries, and at the time Russia was closed to the West. But I want to pass it on to you because it has a real truth in it. It was the story of a prayer meeting in Russia where the doors burst open and two Russian soldiers came in with machine guns. They were shouting, 'We're going to kill the Christians.' The Christians thought the soldiers were drunk but, to their horror, quickly realised that they were stone sober. Then the soldiers said, 'If you're not a Christian, get out.' A number got up and ran. Then the soldiers said to the rest, 'Now can you tell us how to become Christians, please? We had to make sure that we got real Christians so they wouldn't tell on us.' My, a bit of pressure soon sorts out the sheep from the goats!

We are beginning to see some pressure in Britain. Part of the church's future here is suffering, which is the signal, and we are to get ready for it.

We read of the time when there is tremendous pressure on the church, and of the purifying that will follow. When this pressure is taking place, Jesus said, you will have to watch for false prophets at that point. If the danger in the world is false messiahs because the world is insecure, the danger in the church will be false prophets, and we will have to watch them. And you know what false prophets do. They tell of peace, when there is no peace; they try and make things easier for you. I would say that is the fundamental thrust of a false prophet. He cuts down God's standards and accommodates to where the people are, and he seeks to lower moral standards and standards of belief; he tries to keep people happy and he gives them a security other than God. We will have to watch that when the pressure is on.

But the third feature of this signal is to me the most exciting. Jesus then says, *'and the gospel of the kingdom will be preached to all the nations.'* He teaches that the pressure on the church, and the purifying of it that will follow, will get the job done — and the gospel will be preached. I find that exciting, don't you? It may be that God looks down at our groups and thinks: if I put pressure on that group and got it a bit smaller I could reach their town with them. It is a sobering thought, but that is what I hear from this passage, Jesus saying that the pressure will come on the church worldwide, and because of that pressure many will say let's get out. However, the rest will say let's get the job done.

The gospel will be preached to all the nations because with the rest he has an enduring body, and *'he that endures to the end will be saved'* he says. There is going to be a whole salvation in that.

That is the second signal. I do not think it has gone down yet, but I think it is going down, don't you? I see the church under increasing pressure everywhere in the world, and a purifying coming that leaves a group of people who can do the job and who will preach the gospel and evangelise all the nations. Notice the phrase *all the nations* here — persecuted by all the nations, preaching to all the nations. The church has always grown faster when it has been under pressure—just read church history. It grew faster in the first three centuries than it grew for many centuries after that. And is it not exciting to find out that the church in China has been growing during the last few decades? At one stage we thought it must have died out because we were not hearing anything out of that country about it. But under pressure it grew massively.

Now for signal number three. This you will see in the Middle East, and Jesus here refers to the prophet Daniel and to a terrible phrase: the *abomination that causes desolation*. I can only tell you what I understand that means. Daniel refers to it three times and Paul refers to it a number of times as well. I understand by this that one day in Jerusalem itself, the place where God set his name, in the very temple of God, there will be committed the ultimate blasphemy and obscenity: there will be a man in the temple of God who claims to be God—the *man of lawlessness*.

Nothing could cause such an offence to God or be such a cause of suffering to man as a man in Jerusalem claiming to be God — who will say, 'I acknowledge no laws above me; I make all the laws from now on.' It nearly happened 170 years before Jesus, when a man called Antiochus Epiphanes, a Greek emperor, came to Jerusalem, and he walked into the temple where God's holy name had been, and he put on the altar a statue of Zeus, a Greek god, and sacrificed a pig on the altar of God. Pork, on the altar of the Jews. Then he turned the vestries of the temple into brothels. Nothing so shocking had ever occurred in Jewish history and in the city of Jerusalem as the acts of Antiochus Epiphanes, but it is something like that which Paul talks about, and which Jesus talks about. It is something so abominable, so blasphemous, so obscene, so appalling that God will be offended to high heaven, and from that event will come such desolation, such confusion, such suffering, such distress as Jesus says the world has never seen before and will never see again.

That I take to be the 'big trouble', and Jesus says, first, if that were allowed to go on too long nobody would survive. But mercifully God has already said it will be severely limited in time. That is signal number three. So, we can praise God that he is still on the throne and would not let that go on for very long.

But Jesus said the danger during that third signal would be false messiahs and false prophets. Once

40

we have reached signal number three, Satan is going to throw everything he has at us — even with signs and wonders. Now some people are really fooled by signs and wonders; they do not realise that miracles can come from more than one possible source. And Satan will throw the book at us. You will hear all sorts of rumours: Christ is coming, he's over there; Christ is coming, he's over here. There will be silly Christians running around all over the place — catching a bus here, getting a train there, flying somewhere else — because they have heard a rumour. Jesus says do not run anywhere. He said that whenever there is a corpse, vultures gather, and whenever people are panicking you will find Satan and his demonic cohorts. Just do not listen.

I want you to notice that any idea that Jesus has come back secretly is wrong. Jesus says do not listen. He said, actually, *'When I come, it will be like lightning from one end of the heavens to the other.'* Everybody will know immediately. So you do not need to move. Do not move out of your town. Stay right there. You will see; you will know. He will be right there. It is only the panicky people who are misled by the signs and wonders that the devil produces, and by false prophets and false messiahs, who start running around saying, 'It's happened, he's come again, he's come again.' Jesus told us not to listen to them.

There is only one group he told to run, and that is the group that lives in the immediate vicinity of Jerusalem. It is the only group that has to move. And when I was in Jerusalem I had all the Christian leaders together and I pleaded with them to take notice of this. I said, 'If you are alive and still around this city when this happens, don't pack, don't do a thing. Run. Because you'll be right on the doorstep of this wicked, horrid, filthy man who claims to be God. And any of God's people within reach of his arm will have had it, so you'd better run.' That is the only movement there has to be. Any of God's people who happen to be in Jerusalem — if perhaps you are a tourist at that time — you run. Jesus said pray about this. Pray it may not be in the winter when it is cold to hide out in the hills. Pray it won't be on the Sabbath, because there won't be any transport for you. In fact, it will be very difficult to get out of that area if it is in winter or on the Sabbath, especially for pregnant women and nursing mothers. How will they cope?

Jesus said that he was telling his disciples beforehand. He wanted them to know. Now that signal has not gone down yet, but my, can you see it coming? I certainly can. It seems the most possible thing in the world that this should happen, that a man in the Middle East should say, 'I'm God. From now on I make the rules.' He commits that ultimate blasphemy, that abomination in the very city of God.

Let us move to signal number four. After you see signal number three, start looking in the sky for signal number four. I get excited by this. The fourth signal is that immediately after all that trouble, which will be of limited duration, God will turn out every light in the universe. I can remember the first time I was taken to a pantomime, and went into the theatre. We were all excited, and one by one the lights went out so we were sitting in darkness. I had such a sense of anticipation because I knew the next thing would be a blaze of light in front of me and the thing was going to begin. That is what it is going to be like. The last signal is that the sun will go out, the moon will go out, the stars will go out. Every natural light in the universe will be switched off. Suddenly, like lightning, from one end of the heaven to the other, you will hear a tremendous noise.

Some people do not like noise. They think that religion ought to be very quiet and dignified. Well they are going to have problems on this day, because 1 Thessalonians 4:16 is the noisiest verse in the Bible. There is an archangel shouting his head off. There is a trumpet blowing. It is loud enough to raise the dead, a terribly noisy day. But in fact, then you will be able to get ready for your first free trip to the holy land. Then the angels will come and gather the saints.

Notice two things. Up until this point, two things have not happened which some Christians have told me should have happened. Number one, Christ has not come yet — secretly, or any way. And number two, Christians have not gone yet. I think

44

we would need to have heard from Jesus' lips if he had planned to come secretly, or that Christians would go secretly, but he did not teach either. He told us the four signals, and do you know what the big danger is when the fourth goes down, if the danger of the first was false messiahs? If the danger of the second was false prophets and if the danger of the third was false messiahs and prophets, what is the danger of the fourth? Nothing at all. Why not? Because the next event that will happen will be that Jesus is back. So you have no time to worry about false messiahs or false prophets. The prophet will have returned; the Messiah will have come. And the fourth one is just so quick. Well, when you see that lightning, and when the lights go out, you just get ready for lift off!

My grandfather is buried in a graveyard in Newcastle upon Tyne, and on his grave are three words. They are not from the Bible (actually they are from a Methodist hymn that I discovered) but they are on his grave and people sort of scratch their heads and wonder what sort of an odd man is buried under that stone because, after the details of

45

his age and names, the inscription just says, 'What a meeting'. That will be some celebration! There is not a stadium in the world which could hold it. It will have to be in the air to get everybody in, and it will be loud enough to raise the dead, and they will get there first. **That is the centre of the Christian's hope. That is the very heart of our hope for the future.**

There are many other things we hope for — and this does not mean that we wish for it; rather, it means that we look for it in the future. But the heart of it is that the Lord Jesus Christ is coming back to planet earth. That is the heart of it because we know we cannot fully or finally establish the kingdom without the King. England was a commonwealth for one period of its history, under Oliver Cromwell. But there were those who felt it should be a kingdom, and to see that happen they had to get the king back. Charles II had to return. You cannot have a kingdom without the king.

So the heart of our hope is that the King is coming back. Therefore we do not pray a false prayer when we say *your kingdom come, on earth as it is in heaven.* It is a prayer that is going to be answered because the King is coming. And Jesus taught that when you see all these things, you know that he is just the other side of the door. It will be as when you see the fig tree and its leaves beginning to blossom and the twigs getting tender you know summer is just round the corner. Have you noticed how quickly it comes, once the buds have appeared? You are into summer before you know where you are. And Jesus said, *'When you see all these things'* — which means when you see all those signals drop. I do not expect Jesus to come back tonight because those four signals have not dropped, and I am going to trust my eyes not my ears. So I am not going to panic and think I might wake up tomorrow morning and find that others around me have all gone. Nor am I going to think that I will have gone and they will all be here. That is often the other side of that kind of thinking. But I look for those signals, and it is my dearest hope that it will happen in my lifetime, and that they will appear while I am still on earth. That will mean no undertaker will touch this body of mine

or measure me up for a box!   That is the hope of
every generation.

2

THE SEPARATION
AT HIS COMING

(Matthew 25)

But supposing it does not happen in my lifetime? Supposing it is a long way off — how do I adjust to that? So far we have been considering objective knowledge, and we have not thought about how we are to apply it practically. First, we have had to lay this kind of foundation.

We need to know what the signals are. ('Signal' and 'sign' — it is the same word.) What is the sign of the Second Coming and the end of the age? How will we know when it is near? Well, Jesus is just the other side of the door and he said that there are two things that will not pass away, and you can rely on them as proof that these things are going to happen. One is that *'this generation will not pass away'*. But he did not mean that particular group of Jews alive at that time. The word means 'breed', or 'race', so his words meant that the Jews will not disappear before all these things happen. It is clear to me that one of the proofs that what Jesus said about the future is true is he said the Jews would still be around when it happened — and there they are, back in their own nation, in their own land, back in Jerusalem, which is no longer trodden down by Gentiles. That is one of the proofs I know that it will happen.

The second thing is that he said, *'my words will not pass away'*. On the last day of history you will still be able to get hold of a Bible. Other books may pass away. Other men's words will go, but Jesus' words will never pass away. Hanging on to the fact that they are God's people, Israel will never pass away, and God's words through Jesus will never pass away. So I can face the future and read my daily newspaper without panic, and say hallelujah, they are birth pains. They are the contractions of a universe that are going to bring a whole new heaven and new earth, for newborn people with new bodies to live in. I get so excited!

Let me try to summarise in a few sentences the first part of Matthew 24. It began when the disciples asked Jesus about the amazing temple that Herod was in the process of building in Jerusalem. Jesus said that every stone of it would be pulled down. Now, they were sure that no disaster could achieve that, except the end of the world, the end of the age, and the coming of the Messiah. So they asked him specifically when all this would happen, and what the signs or signals of the end of this age, this period of history, would be. They were a little confused because they had not realised the temple would fall long before the end of the age, but Jesus replied giving them four signals we have looked at that would mark his coming, four signs that the end of the age was near. It is getting a grasp of those four that will help you to recognise when the Lord Jesus is coming back. We are to watch for the signals, and these are the four signals he gave us, and there is a clear sequence between them, and there is a clear speed about them — they accelerate. The third comes even more quickly than the second, and the fourth is almost instantaneous. But let us remember the four signs. The first is to be seen in the world, the second in the church, the third in the Middle East, and the fourth in the sky. So we know which direction to look in for the signals. And the first signal in the world was the signal of disasters — wars, earthquakes, famines. We recall Jesus taught that those things were not the end of the world, just the beginning of the birth pains of a new world.

The second signal in the church, you may remember, was that there would be universal persecution, a falling away, a sorting out of church membership by the suffering that would come on the church in every nation; and at the same time a world evangelism, so that as the pressure came on the church in every country, and the church was reduced in size by the pressures on it, it would nevertheless achieve more effectively the evangelisation of the world. As we have already noticed, that has always been proved true. When the church is under pressure it cuts out the passengers on the gospel train, leaving only the crew, and they get on with the job. Signal number three was something appalling happening in Jerusalem, the ultimate blasphemy, a man setting himself up as God in the very place where God put his name, and causing such worldwide troubles and problems and distress that Jesus advises those nearest to him to get out of Judea and run to the hills as fast as they can. A crisis in the Middle East, then, when a man sets himself up as God. If you know your Bible, you will know that this refers to Antichrist, and the distress as the Big Trouble, or the Great Tribulation. We noticed that the Christians have not left, nor has Christ come.

Signal number four, in the sky, was that the sun will be turned off, the moon will be turned off, the stars will be shifted, plunging the whole world into darkness, as the lights in a theatre go down before the curtain goes up — clearing the way for a coming of the Son of Man so glorious that no other light will be needed, and it will be like lightning from east to west. Now those are the four signals, and Jesus said to his disciples that when they saw all these things they would know that he is at the door, just about to step back through into history.

That is the clear teaching of Jesus; I cannot imagine really how many Christians have got so confused about it. Nothing could be clearer: 1, 2, 3, 4 — and when you see all four, you will know that the moment has come. By the time you see all the lights in the sky go out, you just lift up your heads, your day of redemption has come, he is right at the door, just get ready to shout 'hallelujah', and you are off! It is at that point that two men who have worked side by side at the factory bench will say goodbye to each other, and one will go and the other will be left. And two women who have worked in the same kitchen will be separated forever, and one will go and the other be left.

Somebody asked me, 'Do you believe in the rapture?' Of course I do, I just believe that it comes where Jesus said it would come. But I believe there will be a separation, and a gathering of the elect. That is when Jesus said it would happen: after the final signal he will send his angels to gather the elect. Nothing could be clearer, so never get confused about this.

Now we come to the passage which seems to say the opposite, and it is here that confusion may have arisen. Having said *'When you see all these things, you'll know,'* he then says, *'but you don't know, and neither do I. And the angels don't know. In fact, nobody knows except Father, and he is keeping it a secret.'* Which to me is exciting in this sense: that God my Father already has the date in his diary for the coming of Jesus. It is all settled, it is in the calendar, but nobody else knows. Therefore, you must always be wary of anyone who tries to date the Lord's coming. Martin Luther did, and was clearly wrong. John Wesley did, and was wrong. You would be amazed how many great Christian leaders have fallen into the trap of saying it will be such and such a year. Cults also have fallen into that trap. You will find that the Jehovah's Witnesses, the Seventh Day Adventists, and others, have all fallen into the trap of dating the Lord's return, but Jesus said that no-one knows.

I want to write a book on the honesty of Jesus,

because I think his sheer honesty is a greatly neglected aspect of his character. Five times in this passage from Matthew's Gospel that is exactly what we are looking at. Jesus says, *'I tell you the truth'*. One of his favourite words was *Amen*, and he used to begin, not end, sentences with *Amen*. He would begin, *'Amen, Amen I say to you'*; *'verily, verily'*; *'truly, truly, I say to you'*. He was a man who spoke the truth to such a degree that he was able to say, *'I am the truth'*. Therefore, when he did not know something, he was honest enough to admit it. Here is a good example for you. He did not know the date of his return, he was telling his disciples that he could tell them *what* to look for, but not *when*. That is honesty. It behoves every follower of Christ to be equally honest, and no creature can tell you when, but we can say what will take place.

However, that does not resolve the problem, because Jesus seems now to be saying that it will be totally unexpected, it will be like a thief in the night, and that is a favourite phrase of his. It is also used by Peter, it is used by Paul, and it is used by John, right the way through the rest of the New

Testament. They pick this up, that when the Lord comes, he will come like a thief in the night, and that has led many people to say, then surely it will be totally unexpected, surely we will not have any warning at all.

There are two things about a thief coming. The first is obviously that he tries to come secretly, that he tries to come stealthily. The latter is an interesting word, S-T-E-A-L, STEALthily. So a thief tries to come unnoticed. But the second thing about a thief is he is coming to rob you. He is not only trying to come stealthily, he is also coming to steal. Now do you think Jesus is coming to his church to steal from it? Never! Therefore, we raise a question as to whether he is coming to us as a thief. And we shall see that the teaching of the New Testament is perfectly clear: to those who are ready, he will not come as a thief, he will neither come stealthily, nor to steal. But to those who are not ready, it will be totally unexpected, and it will be certain loss. Do you follow me? It is applying the concept of thief to Christians that is the big mistake that has been made. Let me go a little more deeply into this. The tension between, 'you will know when I'm coming,' and, 'you don't know when I'm coming,' is quite wrongly resolved by saying, 'that must mean two comings' — that he must come secretly first and openly second, with a gap in between. That is not the way the New Testament resolves the tension. So what is the answer to this tension whereby Jesus at one minute says, 'when you see these things you will know' and the next minute says, 'but you don't know'? How do you resolve it? There is only one way to resolve it properly, and it is the biblical way. When you do know, it will be too late to get ready. Now that is the only way you can resolve the tension, but it is the right way. In other words, by the time you have seen all the signals and know for sure he is at the door, you will not be able to do a thing about it by then. The time for getting ready will have gone.

That is why you need to be ready, because you do not know when the final signal will drop. It is in that way, not by any silly 'doctrine of two comings', which I cannot find anywhere in the New Testament, as if he is coming secretly for his saints, and openly with them. I cannot find that anywhere. But what I do find is this: those who are not ready will not know at all, just as in the days of Noah they had no idea what was going to happen until they were taken away, and lost everything. Therefore, to those for whom he will come stealthily, he will also come to steal, as a thief in the night. To those for whom it is a complete surprise, it will be utter loss.

Paul teaches in 1 Thessalonians 5 so clearly—

But you, brothers, are not in darkness so that this day should surprise you like a thief. You are all sons of the light and sons of the day. We do not belong to the night or to the darkness. So then, let us not be like others, who are asleep, but let us be alert and self-controlled. For those who sleep, sleep at night, and those who get drunk, get drunk at night. But since we belong to the day, let us be self-controlled, putting on faith and love as a breastplate, and the hope of salvation as a helmet. (NIV) So the whole concept of thieving is a threat only to those who are not ready. But the teaching of Jesus means that to those who are ready it is like a man whose house is going to be burgled, but he gets a tip-off that a thief is on the way, and not only on the way, he knows that it is going to be about one o'clock in the morning. So what does he do? He is ready, and he makes sure that his house is not broken into, he is neither surprised nor robbed. Do you follow Jesus' teaching here? The unexpectedness of it is only for the unready, but those who are ready will be watching, and there will be no secrecy, no surprise, and no loss.

I tell you this, there are people living in our towns now who, when Jesus comes again, are going to lose everything that they value; they are going to lose all the love they have enjoyed, they are going to lose all their possessions, and it will be totally unexpected. It will be like a burglar breaking in. But that should not happen to you, and it need not happen to them. No wonder Jesus says it is like the days of Noah. He was constantly drawing a parallel between what happened in Noah's day and what will happen when he comes back, and therefore, if you dismiss the truthfulness of the Noah story, you are not likely to accept the truthfulness of his coming again. But they are both historical events — one is past, the other is future, but they are terribly similar.

What happened was this. Do you notice that Noah knew what was going to come, but he did not know when? By the time he knew when it would happen, it would have been too late to build an ark, but because he knew what was going to happen for a whole year, he just got on with getting ready. The Canberra was the first ship to be designed on the same proportions as Noah's ark — did you know that? Indeed, most ships since have copied the design. The QE2 was based on the Canberra. The Canberra was the first ship to have the same proportions between beam and length as Noah's ark — Noah discovered that God had the best design for ships. Fascinating! It is real.

God knew that Noah and his three sons could have built that thing in the time they had, but they did not know how much time they had. The important thing was that as soon as Noah knew what was going to happen, he got ready straight away. Then, after a year of building that thing, God told him to get into it, because in seven days the flood would come. So now, at last, he knew when, and it was not a surprise, but it would have been a terrible surprise if he had done nothing to get ready until he knew *when*. He got ready when he knew *what*. I do hope you are following me in this, because I am making a terribly important point. What I am saying is this: from the first part of Matthew 24, it is clear that if we watch for the signals we will know when he is coming. But if you wait until you know when to get ready, you will be far too late. You will be like the foolish virgins we are going to read about in a moment. Oh, they knew what was going to happen, but by the time they knew *when*, it was too late to get ready, and that is the only way I can resolve it. I do not resolve it by having a 'two coming' theory, because I do not believe it to be scriptural. But I do resolve it by saying there are two groups to which he will come: those who will know when it is but who have long since been ready; and those who have not even got ready at all, and to them he will come as a thief, both stealthily and to steal.

Earlier, we referred to Matthew 23:37–24:51 (see above, chapter 1). We continue to read now from 25:1, *NIV*, keeping in mind the closing verses of our earlier quotation.

"At that time the kingdom of heaven will be like ten virgins who took their lamps and went out to meet the bridegroom. Five of them were foolish and five were wise. The foolish ones took their lamps but did not take any oil with them. The wise, however, took oil in jars along with their lamps. The bridegroom was a long time in coming, and they all became drowsy and fell asleep.

"At midnight the cry rang out: 'Here's the bridegroom! Come out to meet him!'

"Then all the virgins woke up and trimmed their lamps. The foolish ones said to the wise, 'Give us some of your oil; our lamps are going out.'

"'No,' they replied, 'there may not be enough for both us and you. Instead, go to those who sell oil and buy some for yourselves.'

"But while they were on their way to buy the oil, the bridegroom arrived. The virgins who were ready went in with him to the wedding banquet. And the door was shut.

"Later the others also came. 'Sir! Sir!' they said. 'Open the door for us!'

"But he replied, 'I tell you the truth, I don't know you.'

"Therefore keep watch, because you do not know the day or the hour.

"Again, it will be like a man going on a journey, who called his servants and entrusted his property to them. To one he gave five talents of money, to another two talents, and to another one talent, each according to his ability. Then he went on his journey. The man who had received the five talents went at once and put his money to work and gained five more. So also, the one with the two talents gained two more. But the man who had received the one talent went off, dug a hole in the ground and hid his master's money.

"After a long time, [that is the third time that phrase has come in here, isn't it?] the master of those servants returned and settled accounts with them. The man who had received the five talents brought the other five. 'Master,' he said, 'you entrusted me with five talents. See, I have gained five more.'

"His master replied, 'Well done, good and faithful servant! You have been faithful with a few things;

I will put you in charge of many things. Come and share your master's happiness!'

"The man with the two talents also came. 'Master,' he said, 'you entrusted me with two talents; see, I have gained two more.'

"His master replied, 'Well done, good and faithful servant! You have been faithful with a few things; I will put you in charge of many things. Come and share your master's happiness!"

"Then the man who had received the one talent came. 'Master,' he said, 'I knew that you are a hard man, harvesting where you have not sown and gathering where you have not scattered seed. So I was afraid and went out and hid your talent in the ground. See, here is what belongs to you.'

"His master replied, 'You wicked, lazy servant! So you knew that I harvest where I have not sown, and gather where I have not scattered seed? Well then, you should have put my money on deposit with the bankers, so that when I returned I would have received it back with interest.

"'Take the talent from him and give it to the one who has the ten talents. For everyone who has will

be given more, and he will have an abundance. Whoever does not have, even what he has will be taken from him. And throw that worthless servant outside, into the darkness, where there will be weeping and gnashing of teeth.'

"When the Son of Man comes in his glory, and all the angels with him, he will sit on his throne in heavenly glory. All the nations will be gathered before him, and he will separate the people one from another as a shepherd separates the sheep from the goats. He will put the sheep on his right and the goats on his left.

"Then the King will say to those on his right, 'Come, you who are blessed by my Father; take your inheritance, the kingdom prepared for you since the creation of the world. For I was hungry and you gave me something to eat, I was thirsty and you gave me something to drink, I was a stranger and you invited me in, I needed clothes and you clothed me, I was sick and you looked after me, I was in prison and you came to visit me.'

"Then the righteous will answer him, 'Lord, when did we see you hungry and feed you, or thirsty and

give you something to drink? When did we see you a stranger and invite you in, or needing clothes and clothe you? When did we see you sick or in prison, and go to visit you?'

"The King will reply, 'I tell you the truth, whatever you did for one of the least of these brothers of mine, you did for me.'

"Then he will say to those on his left, 'Depart from me, you who are cursed, into the eternal fire prepared for the devil and his angels. For I was hungry and you gave me nothing to eat, I was thirsty and you gave me nothing to drink, I was a stranger and you did not invite me in, I needed clothes and you did not clothe me, I was sick and in prison and you did not look after me.'

"They also will answer, 'Lord, when did we see you hungry or thirsty or a stranger or needing clothes or sick or in prison, and did not help you?'

"He will reply, 'I tell you the truth, whatever you did not do for one of the least of these, you did not do for me.'

"Then they will go away to eternal punishment, but the righteous to eternal life."

Here is a heavy word, a critical word, but it is a word that I believe God wants us to hear in this twenty-first century of ours. Here are four stories which all say the same thing, and the emphasis in all four stories is on those who were not ready, and what happened to them. Each of these stories could finish with the sentence, 'and they lived unhappily ever after.' They are not nice stories, they do not finish with all the loose ends being tied up with all the people in a nice, good place; they finish in just the opposite way.

I want to remind you that when Jesus told the stories, he was telling them to twelve men who had been with him for three years. He was not speaking to the crowd, he was not speaking to unbelievers, he was not speaking to the religious leaders of the Jews, he was speaking to those who had followed him, who had eaten with him, walked with him and talked with him. To them he tells these four terrible stories. They follow straight through from all that we have looked at thus far.

Instead of going through the four stories separately, I felt the Lord would have me go through them all together, picking out six features of all four which are the same, so that you get the message. You are probably familiar with the stories, having gone through them yourself, one by one, on your own.

The first thing that is common to all four stories is that they centre around one person, one man, whether it is the owner of the household in the first one, or the bridegroom in the second, or the businessman in the third, or the king in the fourth. And there is no doubt at all that Jesus is speaking about himself — under a variety of headings, as it were. He is saying: I am the one who is in charge of your household; I am your bridegroom; I am your accountant, to whom you will give account; and I am both King and Shepherd. I find it fascinating that he combines shepherd and king in the fourth story, because all the great kings of Israel were shepherds first — have you noticed that? And the shepherd king is an amazing concept, because in the social ladder in the Middle East, the shepherd is at the bottom and the king is at the top. Only God could put those two together. But that is what he used to do. He sent Moses to be a shepherd before he put him into a position of leadership over people. He got David in the fields before he was king. The best kings were at the bottom of the ladder before they got to the top. That is true of Jesus too. He humbled himself even to death on the cross. 'Shepherd King'.

Have you noticed that — throughout this whole discourse — Jesus refers to himself in the third person singular? He does not say, 'I', he always says 'he'. He does not say, 'I am the Son of God,' he says, 'neither the Son,' or he talks about himself as 'the Son of Man', or 'the King'. He never says, 'when I come in my glory with the angels'. Now why should he be so reticent to speak the truth about himself in the first person singular? It is one of the marks of a false messiah that he says, 'I am the Christ.' That is what Jesus warns that false messiahs will say. Instead, Jesus leaves people to find it out for themselves. Here is another profound point to be made: beware of someone who says, 'I am an apostle,' or, 'I am a prophet,' or I am this or I am that. If a man has a genuine gift from God, he never needs to claim it, it will be recognised by others. It is the false prophets and the false Christs who say I am this; I am that. And Jesus speaks about himself quite impersonally, saying when the Christ comes or when the Son of Man comes or when the King does this or when the shepherd does that, or when the householder or when the bridegroom — he does not say 'I'. That is very interesting. There are certain things he does claim about himself in John's Gospel, though: 'I am the bread of life', 'I am the door', 'I am the resurrection and the life'. But none of these concerns pursuit of office or status. They are all functional. So he is not claiming anything for himself, yet all these stories centre around this one person who settles the eternal destiny of everyone who comes before him.

The profound thing we must get hold of here, and which people need to hear, is that one day it will be Jesus who settles their eternal destiny. He has been appointed to do that. In many Anglican churches on Sundays they say, 'from thence he shall come again to judge the quick and the dead'. I wonder if they really believe it. Jesus will settle the question as to where you spend the rest of your existence. It is he who does it. All these four stories centre on him, and it is he who, when he comes, divides people into two groups, and only two — those who are ready, and those who are not. How very striking it is that this is the only division he makes throughout these four stories. He does not go into all the life history, he just asks whether you were ready or not. Because, in fact, the test of your faith as to whether it is real, is whether you are ready. Faith and faithfulness are the same thing in scripture. Faith is not one step that you take one night at an evangelistic crusade, faith is a life you live, and a walk that goes on until you die. Faith is not a one-off thing, it is a continuous thing. It lasts from the moment you first believe to the moment you die, if it is real faith. It becomes faithfulness. Paul did not say, 'Once upon a time on the Damascus road I believed in Jesus, so I'm going to heaven.' No, he would have said: the life I live, I live by faith in the Son of God. And at the end of the road, he said, *I have fought the fight, I have kept the faith*. The only faith that saves is the faith you have at the end of the road. That is the lesson of these four stories: it is faithful faith — well done, good and faithful servant. You believed in me enough to be ready. So we are getting some pretty surprising things out of these four stories.

The second thing that is common to all four stories is this (and I have already mentioned it): in every story a crisis is precipitated by the return of the central figure after a long time. There are those who have said that Jesus thought he would come back very soon indeed, and there are those who have said that the disciples thought that. But in fact Jesus' teaching was plain. In every story he puts in the phrase, *'after a long time'*. And he knew that the long time would be the real test as to whether somebody is ready. If you announce to your town that Jesus is coming back next Thursday, then you might produce a panic reaction fairly quickly, but that will not tell you that they are ready. The people who are really ready can cope with a long wait. Far too often we have used, 'he might come next Thursday', to try to get people ready. That is false motivation and it does not produce people who are ready, because if he does not come next Thursday they are more unready than ever by next week. The people who are really ready are ready if he comes tomorrow or in a thousand years. They would still be ready. But it is his coming that produces the crisis, and divides people into those two groups.

Let us move on to the third point. In all these four stories some people were ready, and we may ask *how* were they ready? And each of the four stories tells us something different here, but we can put them all together. In the first story, the man was ready because he had got on with the job he had been left to do. That is the first way in which he was ready. There is an old Negro spiritual song which I love, and it goes like this:

There's a king and a captain high,
and he's coming by and by,
and he'll find me hoeing cotton when he comes.
You can hear his legions charging
in the regions of the sky,
and he'll find me hoeing cotton when he comes.
There's a man they thrust aside,

who was tortured 'til he died,
and he'll find me hoeing cotton when he comes.
He was hated and rejected,
he was scorned and crucified,
and he'll find me hoeing cotton when he comes.
When he comes, when he comes,
he'll be crowned by saints and angels
when he comes.
They'll be shouting out hosanna
to the man that men denied,
and I'll kneel among my cotton when he comes.

In other words, I'll get on with the job! There have been Christians, though, who got so caught up with the Second Coming that they left their jobs. I have actually had to counsel some who said 'The Lord is so near that I just want to get on with this' — and they were panicking. 'And you'll find me hoeing cotton when he comes.' If you cannot understand what I am saying, you may never see God's purpose in your daily work. But, you see, the best thing you can do to get ready for his coming is to get on with the job he told you to do, whether that job is to be a church leader, or to be a butcher or a housewife, or to work at a factory bench. *'Blessed is that servant whom his master finds so doing.'*

In the second story they were ready because they had built up enough resources for the future to carry on for some time. Now, there are some Christians who are terribly keen on any short-term project. You know, the latest thing in missionary work is to go overseas for a very short time. A dear old missionary was discussing the change in missionary work. Somebody asked him, 'What's the biggest change in missionary work between when you went out and today?' His reply was, 'I'll tell you, we went out to stay.'

Sticking at it means building up resources, not using them up. The five wise virgins had built up their resources so that even though there was a long delay, they could carry on. The simple fact is that they knew they would need their lamps inside the wedding, as well as after the bridegroom came. That is the point of the story, because they did not have electric light in those days, and when you went to a wedding everybody brought a lamp to light up the whole wedding, to help with the celebration. So they did not just need lamps while they were in the street, they needed those lamps after the bridegroom came, and they built up their resources to do something for the bridegroom after his coming. The others, though, were just looking for the bridegroom, they were not building up any resources, and therefore they could not do anything after he came. They were not ready. The reward for serving God faithfully is not a large, comfortable sofa in heaven, with RIP embroidered on it, it is more work, it is serving. And it is those who have built up their resources for what happens after the bridegroom comes who are ready.

The third story tells us that if God has invested anything in us, he is expecting interest back. He is expecting you to multiply your gift — and if you use your gift, it will multiply. If a preacher uses his gift, others will be inspired into preaching. If a singer uses her gift, others will be inspired into singing. Whatever gift you use, it inspires others to use their gift too, thereby multiplying it. Isn't it interesting that it was the man with only one talent whose attitude was: well, it's not worth doing much with my little gift when everybody round me has so many more — and he buried it. He was not ready. Those who are ready are those who increase the investment God has put in them.

The fourth thing is that those who are ready are those who are caring for the needs of Christ's brethren. And his brethren are not neighbours – that is too wide an interpretation – nor are they the Jewish nation, for that is too narrow an interpretation. I believe the word 'brethren' always meant the same thing when Jesus used it. 'Go and tell my brethren'; 'Whoever is my brother is the one who does the will of my Father.' In other words, to do something for a believer is actually to serve Jesus.

A famous preacher went to visit and preach in Yorkshire once, and he stayed in a wealthy home. A maid in the kitchen was sent to the butcher to get a joint of meat for the weekend. And she said to the butcher, 'Oh, the fuss that's being made about this preacher.' She said, 'The things we're having to do to get ready for him.' She said, 'You'd think

Jesus Christ himself was coming, the way they're carrying on.' A week later she went back to the butcher, and the butcher remembered her words, and he said, 'Well, did Jesus come and stay in your house?' She said 'yes'. She had been led to the Lord by the preacher over the weekend, and she knew in serving him she was serving Jesus. If you give a cup of cold water to another Christian, you have given Jesus a drink. What an amazing concept that is. And those who are ready are those who are realising that to serve a brother of Jesus is to serve him. To laugh at a brother of Jesus is to laugh at Jesus. To make fun of a brother Christian is to make fun of Jesus. *'Whatever you do to the least . . . .'*

These four stories have in common that those who are ready are rewarded. But the reward is rather different from what we might expect. In the first story, the reward for being faithful is greater responsibility. If you do a good job in the church then you will get more jobs. Never be surprised at that, because it is the reward of Jesus. We think, 'Just because I did that well, now they're on to me about this.' But that is the reward. Which means that the reward is not something different from what you have done, it is not like a spoonful of jam after you have swallowed a pill. So if you are not enjoying serving the Lord, you had better watch out or you will not get a reward. Do you follow me? The reward is not rest, but more work.

Of course, the world thinks differently. The world says, 'Well, I've worked forty years in this factory, I deserve a good retirement now.' Jesus does not offer retirement as a reward, he offers promotion. A scientist worked for years in a laboratory — it was a very rough laboratory, a garden shed really — but he managed to discover a medical answer to a disease that really has affected the world. So the world got together — or at least those who knew of it — to reward him, and they thought, 'Now what can we reward him with?' They built him a new laboratory, and that was his reward —and that is the kind of reward Jesus gives. In the second story there is the opportunity to celebrate, to enter into a joyful celebration — that is the reward. In the third story, it is both the first and the second mixed together, it is promotion and entering into joy. And in the fourth story, it is actually to reign with Christ on a throne, to enter into a kingship prepared. I love that word 'prepared', because Jesus is teaching here: if you have prepared for me, I have prepared for you. *'I go to prepare a place for you.'* Are you preparing yourself for heaven as much as Jesus is preparing heaven for you? There are two sides to being prepared.

There is a further thing that these stories have in common, and here we are coming near to the burden for this section. In each of the four stories, some were not ready. The whole point of these stories is that some were not ready, and the shock that I got when I asked in what sense they were not ready was this: they were not ready because they had not done certain things. They were not criminals, they were not full of vice, there was not a murderer or an adulterer among them. In fact, none of them is accused of a single vice or a single crime or a single sin. They are only accused of having not done something. Now that is a shock. Again, in some Church of England buildings in the country on Sundays, people will recite the General

Confession, saying, 'we have left undone those things which we ought to have done'. Do you know that a man can go to hell not because of what he has done, but because of what he did not do? The common defence against accusation is, 'Well, I've never done anybody any harm' — but that is not an adequate defence plea, because God can reply: but you never did anybody any good, either. Not doing any harm is not adequate. I gave you life, I gave you talents, I gave you opportunities, and you did nothing with them. Now that is the shock of these four stories. Remember, Jesus is speaking to disciples, warning them of the danger of doing nothing. In fact, to get to hell, that is all you need to do — nothing. That is the teaching of Jesus.

In the first case a man had been left to give food to the other servants and he had not given it. In the second case, they were supposed to have enough oil to light the wedding, and they had not got it. In the third case, the man with one talent had failed to improve it. He had not spent it on himself, he had not gone out and stolen his master's money and indulged himself —he just had not done anything with it. In fact, in the fourth case (*You never visited me, you never clothed me, you never gave me a drink*) they really gave the whole game away by the tone of their response. Oh, Lord, if we'd realised it was you — what social snobbery lies in that implication! In other words: Oh, we thought it was just some unimportant person. If we had known it was you, if we had known it was important, we would have done it. Isn't that awful? The sins of neglect, what are called the sins of omission, are what Jesus is talking about here — not the bad things we have done, but the good things we have not done. Now that is a serious word.

The final thing that there is in these four stories is this: the unready are punished. They are not forgiven — not one of them. They are not given a second chance — not one of them. The simple fact is that when the Lord comes back again, the chances are over. The door is shut; there is no appeal, the decision is final. For a number of years I have found myself getting less and less able to enter into Christmas. I am afraid that I find myself refusing to preach over Christmas — I just cannot bring myself to do it. The reason for this change is that if I did I would want to preach on the Second Coming of the Lord. That is what people need to hear, and it is a wise church that has put Advent just before Christmas, because those who observe Advent preach the Second Coming of Christ just before Christmas. The world does not mind a baby in a manger, because they think that the baby is not going to judge them. The world does not mind the First Coming of the Lord, because that was for forgiveness and mercy and salvation. The world loves the First Coming of Jesus, and hates the Second Coming. Therefore, the world will celebrate his First Coming until the last Christmas, but they will not celebrate his Second Coming, because he is not coming again to save the world. 'From thence he shall come again to *judge* the quick and the dead'. And it is not very nice to be told that you are going to be judged for what you have not done. The world will never celebrate that, but it is as true as his First Coming. As an aside, it struck me that you do not need so much faith to believe he is coming the second time when he has been once. It is much easier to believe he will come again, isn't it?

Now look at the punishment that was meted out to those who were not ready. Cut to pieces, weeping and gnashing of teeth, shut outside, in the outer darkness, weeping and gnashing of teeth again, cursed, eternal fire, eternal punishment. I just cannot get round those words of Jesus. I am amazed that the only person in the whole Bible that God could trust with the truth about hell was Jesus. He could not trust any apostle with the truth, he could not trust any prophet with the truth. All my teaching on hell comes from Jesus, as if the one person who could warn people about it would be the one who would give his own blood to save people from it. Here we have the profound truth spoken, and we have got to grapple with this very serious truth that Jesus is giving us — that disciples who are not ready go to hell. It is disciples that he is talking to, and disciples who are not ready go to hell. There is no trace here of purgatory, there is no trace here of being 'handicapped' in the future life. There is only the language which Jesus reserved for hell, which is a place of most appalling suffering

— weeping and gnashing of teeth. I used to think that this would be remorse, but I now realise it is also rage, and that hell will be full of raving people who are shaking their fists at God for sending them there. And I would not like to be surrounded by a lot of raging people who are angry with God for sending them there. Weeping and gnashing of teeth, outer darkness — it is terrible.

I do not think people inside the church always realise — people outside the church certainly do not realise — who Jesus is talking to or what he is saying. So we must finally face very honestly the truth of what Jesus is saying. These are not rank unbelievers, these are not pagan, heathen people on some distant island, these are twelve men who for three years had shared his ministry. These are twelve men who had taught and preached and healed in the name of Jesus. And in each of the stories, the people who are finally rejected are those who have had a connection with the central figure in the story. In the first story it is a servant of the householder who is sent to hell. In the second story it is five of the virgins, the bridesmaids, waiting for the wedding, looking for the bridegroom coming. In the third story it is a man who has been given a talent by the businessman before he went on the journey. And in the fourth story, the goats have been in the flock of the one shepherd. This is the challenge of these four stories. You can be so near to Jesus and still not be ready. And I am very close now to the burden the Lord gave me for you in this book. We are not talking about the people out there in our respective towns and the danger they are in now, we are talking about the danger each of us as Christians is in.

So how can we be ready? What was wrong with those who were not ready? What was the root of their failure? Why did they not make it? The answer is two-fold. Firstly, their relationship with the Lord was inadequate. They did not know him, but he knew about them perfectly. They thought they knew him, but they did not. Think of the man with one talent, and he came and he said, *'O Lord, I knew you were a hard man. You make your money out of other people's labour.'* A typical man who does not like working for other people. You have heard people talk like this, haven't you? 'Why should he make a profit on my labour?' It is almost a shop steward talking here. In effect he is saying: you are a hard man, and I was afraid that if I took the risk and lost your money I would really get it in the neck. So I didn't take any risks because I knew you, you see. I knew what you're like, you're a hard master, you're just after grabbing some money. But he did not know the master. The master wanted to share his joy, the master wanted to give talents, thereby handing people more responsibility. The master wanted to share everything he had with the servants. That was the kind of man he was. But this man who buried his talent said: *Oh I know you.* He did not at all. Do you understand this? If we are serving the Lord because we think he is hard, and because he pushes us, and because he makes us do it, we do not really know him. He is doing it so that he may share more responsibility with you, so that he may say, *'Well done, good and faithful servant, come and share my joy.'* That is why he is doing it, not because he is hard, because he wants to drive you, but because he wants to share with you. You see, you do not know the Lord unless you understand his character. If you know what he is really like, you will turn your ten talents into ten more, your five into five more, your two into two more; and even your little one you will turn into one more, if you know him. But they did not know him. In fact, the bridegroom says to those foolish virgins, *'I don't know you.'*

The second thing which was wrong with those who were not ready was this: not only was their relationship with Christ the Lord inadequate, their relationship with his brethren was also inadequate. Not only did he not recognise them (*'I don't know you'*), but they had not recognised him. They were asking when they had seen him, and he could tell them they had seen him many, many times, because when you meet with fellow Christians you have seen the Lord Jesus. You just need to look around and you have seen him, and you could give him a meal at that point. Do you recognise him? If you do not recognise him in each other, don't you dare take bread at the Holy Communion, because if you cannot discern the body, you should not eat that bread — you would be sick, and even die.

When you look around, can you discern Jesus? Do you recognise him? Do you know him in your fellow Christians? In other words, those who are ready are those who have a good relationship with the Lord and a good relationship with his brethren — that is all — and out of that will grow all the other things. Out of that will grow a desire to multiply talents; out of that will grow a desire to build up resources; out of that will grow a faithful feeding of his household; out of that will grow the service and the meeting needs. It will all grow out of those two things.

As I prepared this message, my burden was this: how many in our churches are just hanging on, just fellow travellers who have only come along for the celebration because it is big, noisy and exciting, and are just tagging along with the communities? I tell you, under pressure we would soon find out. I just felt the Lord was saying, 'Don't assume that because you are singing about my coming again, you are ready. Don't assume, because you have joined yourself to the flock, that you are a sheep.

Don't assume, because you are among the virgins waiting for the bridegroom, that you are a wise virgin. Don't assume, because you are listening to others use their talents, that you are using your talent. Do not assume anything, but get to know your Lord and get to know his brethren. Recognise him in each other and get ready.'

Now some readers would come straight at me saying, 'Do you believe once saved, always saved?' I preach on Jesus' word, and you must take Jesus' word as it stands, and I believe it is possible to be a disciple and to go to hell. My proof? Out of the twelve men, there was one who did not make it, who was listening to these words, who had gone out preaching and healing in the name of Jesus, who had left all to follow him, who was part of the inner body of the twelve, and he was listening to these stories. He was the treasurer, and he did not know Jesus well enough to realise that Jesus knew he was fiddling the books. He was faithless in looking after the money of the church. The first church treasurer was crooked. And Jesus, I am quite sure, as he told these four stories, kept looking at Judas, wondering, will you be ready? But Judas was not. And Judas went and hanged himself — it says he went to his own place. He is the only one of those disciples I do not expect to see in heaven. But then in even saying that, I am being presumptuous about myself.

So it is a sobering word I bring you in this book, it is a word that will challenge all sorts of traditional ideas, it will challenge all sorts of complacency. We can turn our complacency into doctrine, we can say, 'It's okay, I've got my ticket to glory.' We can say, 'It's okay, the Christians are all going to be snatched up before the big trouble.' We can turn all our human hopes into doctrines, but I go by the word of Jesus, and I take Jesus' word at its face value. And Jesus wants disciples in your town and my town who will be ready, who know what is coming, but who are getting prepared now, so that when he does come it will not be too late. You will not have time to build an ark then.

A dear old Scottish man who was dying and was visited by the minister to get him ready for his death, said, 'You don't need to, I thatched my house when the weather was warm.' He did not need a minister to visit him as he lay dying.

Here is a final sentence from St Augustine: 'He who loves the coming of the Lord is not he who affirms it is far off, nor is it he who says it is near, but rather he who, whether it be far or near, awaits it with sincere faith, steadfast hope and fervent love.' Now read that again, and absorb it.

PRAYER

Father, I tremble in your presence at such a word, because I know it applies to every one of us, and that you are speaking to your disciples at this time, and telling us to use this time to be ready, so that whenever you come you may find us doing the work you gave us to do. And Lord, I pray particularly that my knowledge of you — and of other Christians — may be deepened, so that out of that intimate relationship may flow a readiness to serve, a readiness to improve my talents, a readiness to be totally involved and totally committed. I ask it in Jesus' name. *Amen.*